THE NIGHTS ALSO

THE NIGHTS ALSO

ANNA SWANSON

POEMS

Tightrope Books

Tightrope Books
602 Markham Street
Toronto, Ontario
Canada M6G 2L8
www.TightropeBooks.com

Canada Council
for the Arts Conseil des Arts
du Canada

EDITOR: Shirarose Wilensky
COPY EDITOR: Chris Edwards
COVER DESIGN: Karen Correia Da Silva
TYPESETTING: Shirarose Wilensky

ONTARIO ARTS COUNCIL
CONSEIL DES ARTS DE L'ONTARIO

Produced with the assistance of the Canada Council for the Arts and the Ontario Arts Council.

Printed in Canada.

LIBRARY AND ARCHIVES CANADA CATALOGUING IN PUBLICATION

Swanson, Anna, 1974-
    The nights also / Anna Swanson.

Poems.
ISBN 978-1-926639-13-0

    I. Title.

PS8637.W35N54 2010   C811'.6   C2010-900560-0

CONTENTS

CALLING OUT THE WRONG NAME IN BED

THE THIN EDGE OF STILLNESS

The days of your life might mean only the days;
all the days of your life includes the nights also.

—BEN ZOMA, MISHNAH BERAKHOT 1:5

The nights also

Not only the lake like this, not only the low sun cutting the mist, and those
three smooth ripples each side of the silent bow
    but the nights also

Not only the microphone, the acceptance letter, the applause, the wide place
past the treeline where we finally understand why we've come all this way

Not only the life we claim on our tax returns, not only the breakroom gossip,
the lost umbrellas, the small triumphs of public transit

Not only the dreams we fortress with sandbags of will

Not only the ways we touch each other in public

Not only what we hang on the wall, what we polish for the in-laws, what we
sort, schedule, tabulate, catalogue, and account for

Not only what we understand

BETWEEN SLEEP AND SLEEP

Lullaby for small

What do I know of the world these days?
This room, the merciful windows
and whatever weather hits them. The world is
this: the eagles calling out into the sleepless night,
and me, small enough to fit in a coat pocket.
There is a box I keep on the table by my bed.
A box just large enough for all the doctors'
perfect remedies. The eagles call out into the night,
the falling notes of their cries like ripples around a pebble,
which has disappeared into dark water.
At five, a peacock walks the ledge
outside my bedroom window. The light
begins so slowly. And me, curled in my bed,
small enough to fit in a coat pocket.
I have worn out my anger, and there is not much
of me left. I want the backseat
of our old orange Datsun. I want my father
to carry me in. I swore I'd never get too big.
Sleep, baby, sleep. All the old songs.
Thy father tend the sheep. I want
                              shhhhh.
The falling notes like ripples. The pebble.
The dark water closing around it.

Oh dear body

I have dug down through loam, clay, gravel, bones.
If I look back up, I can see the path out of here:
bones, gravel, clay, loam, sky. Yesterday,
I hit water. Suddenly I am nothing more
than a woman floating in a well.
Oh dear body, you who were once a green oak
in which the sap was made of birds—
How did we get here?
The sun makes its arc across the mouth
of this hole. I search the small circle of sky
for clouds, for the rain on whose back
I might return to the world.

Symptom #1: Fatigue

Fatigue takes
you down the hall,
opens the one door
you've tried so cleverly
to hide, throws you in there
with an old mattress. The walls
are made only of wallpaper and the
layers keep curling in on you. You reach around
with a brush full of glue, trying to keep the paper walls
together, while she goes out, two-stepping
with your future.

Descent

Victoria, you call it, but that's only a coin landing language-side down. This is a country that admits no tourists. *Moss Street, Fernwood, Fairfield, Dallas Road.* All the same street signs, the government buildings, the birds circling where the untreated sewage rises up beside the breakwater. You can walk to the ocean. But that's only part of the long descent.

If you live in Victoria, the place you arrive at is called Victoria. The path there is a street parade dressed up like your life. Look—here's your bedroom closet painted on a cardboard box. It shuffles along next to the big bay window, and that perfect little telephone with the feet of a rat. You keep walking and walking just to keep up with your bed.

At the end of your street there is a giant sculpture of a reclining mattress cast in concrete, as if that were the only way to keep it from walking away. *Art*, you call it, although a less generous word would do. *Representation*, you call it, as if it weren't somebody else's emergency. Across the street, they are building an apartment tower using only turquoise insulation, staple guns, and plastic sheeting. On the sidewalk out front, the last few leaves of the Japanese maples are backlit by the cold sun. *Fall*, you call it. What else can you do?

The illness clause

excerpts from the literature of illness

If illness was only at the level of the physical

If illness was caused by bacteria or other pathogens

If illness was perceived to be under control

If illness was the reason behind a somewhat lacklustre performance

If illness was from sin and sin was caused by demons

If illness was just the signal a healthy body sent to urge clarification of your thoughts

If illness was etiologically related to depression

If illness was not randomly distributed across the population

If illness was perceived as serious

If illness was seen to be an individual response to unhealthy lifestyles

If illness was the result of uncontrollable forces

If illness was a central—the central—theme

If illness was incurable

If illness was not recorded

If illness was due to the spirit having fled the body

If illness was reported on the medical questionnaire

If illness was no legal excuse

If illness was a nagging worry

was widespread

was rampant

was suspected

was the cause

was known

If illness was occurring

was occurring

was occurring

Symptom #6: Poor concentration

The mind
tries knitting:
two roofing hammers
counting aloud,
knit one, purl two.
The mind takes up carpentry
and spends the day
pounding nails with
a handful of lint. The mind
sits at the desk with
the morning's mail, turns over
each crisp envelope. Sighs. Picks up
the old knife made of porridge.

Sestina for my name

We sat on the kitchen floor around eighty pounds of asparagus,
preparing for winter. Most of us strangers. A theatre student
told us why we find it hard to remember names.
The secret, she said, is to listen when people are introduced,
but most of us don't because we're scared we'll forget
our own names. Instead of listening—*Hi, I'm Anna. Anna.*—

we practise in our heads. *Nice to meet you, I'm Anna.*
We sat in a circle on the floor, bent the asparagus,
and let it snap where it would. We slowly forgot
our city speed. A pile of spears. A pile of blunt ends. We studied
with our hands. Bent and snapped our way through introductions.
Laughed when we caught ourselves practising names.

We learned about the lives attached to the names:
the pottery, the geology research, the dance auditions. Then, *Anna.*
They looked up, waiting for me to introduce
my days. I wondered as I sat there, snapping asparagus,
what it was I did—teacher, artist, accountant, grad student.
I never imagined this was something I could forget.

How much we store against forgetting
in the small cubbyholes of our lives. The least of it our names.

But I remember the minutes when it all went missing. I study
that gap, that place between maps, when all I had was *Anna,*
and the hope that what I did was useful or beautiful. Beyond the asparagus,
I could think of no other life. A strange introduction

to the years that were to come. Even as illness introduces
us to the world under the skin of the world, there is still more to forget.
But there are days when we become bakers-of-bread, benders-of-asparagus,
shovellers-of-snow. Something thinner. We forget to practise our names
and the world rushes into the pause. Where a name would be,
a mouthful of wind. What could I learn if I became a student

of this space? Maybe nothing. This is the way with students.
I was sick for six years and can't tell you what I learnt. I avoided introductions
because I had nothing to say. But there was something underneath even *Anna,*
which never disappeared. I may never have a word for it. Even when I forgot
how to be a climber, a paddler, a planner of parades. Even when all the names
I had for myself broke away, easy as ends of asparagus.

I keep returning to the asparagus day. Study the bend and snap of my life,
the thin fissure between me and my name. But each time I introduce myself,
I can't forget the old fear. *Anna. Hello, my name's Anna. Anna. I'm Anna.*

Argument for remembering

Because people said, *But you look great*

Because I was afraid I might never sleep again

Because I remember the first time I had to ask a man to move a table for me

Because I dropped all my courses but one so I'd have something to say when people asked me what I did

Because the doctor at the clinic told me I was lazy and it would help if I washed more often

Because, being my mother's daughter, I followed him and repeated what he had said back to him loudly in front of an entire waiting room, and in his couriered letter of apology the doctor said it looked to him as if my hands were dirty, but in retrospect it may just have been the colour of my skin

Because everyone asks me what I did, but what I did was nothing

Because: welfare forms, disability benefits applications, request to withdraw from classes after the drop date forms, doctor's notes, proof of rent forms, bank records, personal statements

Because sometimes I looked through my address book to remember who my friends were

Because I went out dancing when I knew I would spend three days in bed afterwards

Because: homeopathy, Chinese herbs, acupuncture, food testing, melatonin, Siberian ginseng, iron supplements, body temperature tracking, caffeine, bio-kinetic muscle testing, pretending I was okay, counselling, rest, and thirty-nine blood tests in one day

Because I still can't say why I got better when I did

Because I remember climbing before I got sick, that day halfway up Neat and Cool, at the crux with one heel reaching above my head, when one of our friends turned to my boyfriend and said, *Fuck she's strong*

Because I can't go back to being the person I was before I got sick

Because I wouldn't choose to

Because I get scared any time I feel tired for more than two days in a row

Because I never realized that when people ask us who we are, we answer with what we do

Symptom #11: Sleep may be disturbed

No sleep and, after eighty-nine days, God
gets frustrated too, fills a cardboard piano box
with cement, and drops it. There is compression,
you know that, forced exhalation
so strong it turns turbines in the sky,
powers up a small city of appliances.
Then everything sputters and goes out.

You are through the bed, flattened
to the floor. You are one molecule thick.
You are pinned to the bedrock below the house.
You have no breath, no terror, no dreams.
Some would call this sleep,
but you know it's something
holier. In the morning, the fog
you've walked through for weeks
has been pressed back into objects:
the alarm clock, the cordless phone,
the ivory sickle on your desk
waiting for the morning mail.

The Patron Saint of Bagpipes

The Patron Saint of Bagpipes and the Patron Saint
of Concerned Parents are having at it
at last. Gathered around, cussing and cheering,
are the patron saints of adult acne, late periods,
of slot machines, locking the keys in the car, of calling
out the wrong name in bed. And, of course,
the patron saint of trying to fall asleep
when you're lonely. These are the lesser saints
in their lesser heaven, blessed only with the power
to hold back your hair while you puke
in your private stall. They gather round,
waiting, as Our Lady of the PTA
threatens to get all fisticuffs with Bagpipes.
Bystanders become a crowd, and the crowd
starts to circle. Perhaps, I tell myself, perhaps

this is why they can't hear me. Tonight, when I've called
everyone in my book, when I've asked that thin thread of faith
to show itself like fishing line against the dark lake.
No matter what small thing I ask for—waiting poised
to close myself over any flash or morsel—no one answers.
So, as I drift into that place that isn't sleep,
I lay my money down and buy Pipes another pint,

sidle up behind PTA and whisper loudly—
Thinks he can intimidate her. I know, and especially
after how he's been eyeing her daughter.
Then I join the crowd.

Mattress songs

take off all the pretty sheets:
old mattress   same old
cloth metal quicksand
same old   rustybones sorrow
quick quick someone please
invent fitted sheets and featherbeds
thread-count thread-count la-la-la-la crazy quilts someone please
      duvet covers linen sets
         don't make me look
            at my naked days   don't

hips
you know hips meant to be
more than a pressure-point
more than a sore place pressing into a mattress
hips meant for
shift   flex
what hips want is:
circumnavigate bass notes in a bar

not this hips hiding
like the light
hurts

oh this head-rock
this failed meteor
unignited weight
shaper-of-pillows
oh you onetrickhunter holding a small sky's
worth of bird feathers
pinned
to a mattress

mattress made of tired frogs
all crouch and sink
no leap
      no leap
            no more
leap
but some nights they
come alive

squirm
out from under my dream-weight
suck down bedside-cup-water
ricochet off walls like swamp rockets smash themselves
against the ceiling yes
yes
but not

often

knees
not frogs not
doors that swing open
knees like broken scissors on the mattress
like some old trash useless cutlery
some bottom drawer forgotten things
bent yes
but not bending
not dancing the up down
not springboard songs not frogs
not knees not

today

lie down
let sleep come
like a woman who almost
loves you
make you an offer
you can't refuse

stay awhile

✧

when did I become a
      hollow in a bed
me and my mattress-shadow
the days just a quick gravity trick
an exercise in
         leap   leap
                remember
come   back   down
mattress missing me
missing mattress-shadow me

✧

we ten of us once
we took a mattress
tobogganing
footed with crazy-carpets
was the fastest damn mattress in the world
not springs but
                shocks
not sleep but
                dreams

The logic of trains

You've learned when it gets like this
to make your nights into railcars—
each one a small victory
against here. The days
are gaps between cars,
are whatever is lost
in the thud of coupling
before you leave the station
and speed sleeping past
towns you won't see.
You would give them freely,
these days, for a full fare
out of here. If you could wake up
already elsewhere, you would.
But each day, each day is a
thin steel catwalk of light

that must be crossed.
The tracks below are a fast-passing
stillness along which you dare
not trail your fingers.
The wind is bright and always against you.
This is the logic of trains.

You understand your days
as a necessary risk:
that short un-walled leap
between sleep
and sleep.

Away from here

She sits on the bank where the delta opens its mud flats to the sea. By the shore, an old tree. All day she has watched the herons make their quiet landings, curl in on themselves like new leaves. At dusk they are the colour of branches.

There is a period of still. She waits. Then a shadow startles, stretches out of itself, spreads its wide wings. It shakes off some accumulation, and slices into the sky. *There is no word but beauty*, she thinks, watching wing tips like wet knives in their slow arc. When the wings close down, it is hard to breathe, and as the wings rise up she sucks in the thin air of which there is never enough.

Some nights, one movement will stir the whole tree into flight. Wings fling themselves open, one after another. Each bird pauses on the edge of a branch just long enough for her to see what is leaving.

It takes strong hands to stay open when beauty gets this sharp. She watches the birds scatter in the almost dark: wide, slow, painfully precise. Her every tendon aches. The strange angle of their necks, their long heads reaching into the night as if following the very last of the light away from here.

Any meaning

The meanings given to symptoms and distress can transform suffering. Meaning—any meaning—serves to turn back the tide of chaos and bafflement that confronts us in affliction.
—LAURENCE J. KIRMAYER

If illness was a mortgage, did it get paid off quicker the sicker we were?

If illness was an exercise machine, how many calories did we burn a year?

If illness was an endangered animal, did we give a damn?

If illness was a cheap motel, did we care as long as we were getting laid?

If illness was a fistfight, were we friends again when the hangover wore off?

If illness was a train wreck, did we finally find out what goods we've been hauling all this way?

If illness was boot camp, did we have well-defined souls?

If illness was a reality show, did anyone watch?

If illness was a ping-pong match, were those my days that kept flying past me full of air?

If illness was your bright idea, could I please see you in my office *right now*?

If illness was a child, will anyone ever love it enough?

Four years and finally getting better

It's that moment, hours later, when I realize
I'm still driving as if only the bottom
few inches of the windshield were
clear. That's how it feels.
I made myself so small,
the steering wheel in the way of everything,
me thinking the glass was
what there was.

How it could be: Walking

Feet tender and vicious as mouths
on the pavement.
Hips a hinge hungry
for distance. Two legs
that devour the space between,
pumping from open
to open again.
Beautiful boots.
Beautiful bone-filled legs.
How they hang from the pelvis
like unstoppered scissor blades—
no dull edge. And the will,
deep in the well
of organs, flexing
like a hand.

The moment

When the world says *Go*. When everything
turns green: the neon signs, the on-ramps,
the sun rising like an oversized traffic light
across the highway. I've left the muffler
on the side of the road. I've cut off the roof.
I'm speeding down sunburnt tarmac.
To have a body. To move
from inside the skin. I remember now.
To pivot around a paddle into white water.
To somersault, to hipcheck, to handspring.
To nail a baseball into a glove. To reach
past safety and smack against joy.
I remember. To jackknife
off the wharf into cold water.
To wake up. To wake up and want
to start the day. This body:
the green sap rising.

Answer from silence

If it isn't in the Talmud, the scholars say,
then perhaps we should think about why.
Illness. Illness, and all I ever wanted
was to understand. Each day I break again
on the shore of no good goddamn reason.
They call it the answer from silence.
What, then, do I make of these six years?
I wanted to know where the thin ribbons
of meltwater might someday meet.
I wanted a theory that would make it
through the night. I wanted—
it was so simple—to know why.

But all God ever said to me was
something about a girl and a bicycle,
the rush of sun through the alders.
Oh, and the hill, the hill.
I think that was the important part.

CALLING OUT THE WRONG NAME IN BED

Loose woman

I figured it was like the difference between skinny-dipping and going swimming at the rec centre. Too many times I stood on a diving board in an old bathing suit that was never enough to cover all the right places, especially if you didn't shave, and I didn't. Always an aquafit class somewhere and a gym full of people behind a glass wall at the side of the pool. No one was looking at me but it felt like they were all watching, because everyone there was always watching. And is it any wonder I never learned to dive as though my body were beautiful?

The first time I swam naked in daylight there were thirty of us. Imagine it. Enough naked women to sink a small dock. I swam out from the others and floated on my back. With the sun on my skin, I felt my muscles release, let my arms and legs loosen. Slowly I learned the lake would still hold me if I let go like this, my mouth barely above water and my breasts perfect islands beside a blooming continent of belly. I opened my thighs to the ripples that women's bodies were making somewhere, until my limbs made a star and I was looking up at the sky. The clouds moved so easily. Later someone said, *You looked beautiful out there.* And I believed her. That was the summer I learned to dive like I meant it: every arcing part of me.

Shirt collar

You're standing by the mirror,
and I watch your fingers
slip cufflinks through buttonholes.
Your shoulders ease back,
as if the world finally has room for them,
as if your skin fits differently
under this shirt. Your small breasts
press out, unexpected
in these starched folds.

For you I would learn
the forgotten motions of my father's hands,
the foreign ritual of folding a tie
in on itself, anything
for an excuse to reach behind your neck,
slide my fingers up under your shirt collar,
that sharp cool crease.

Tulip

The tulip starts out all knee socks, headbands,
good posture. There is an elegance that grows out of this:
flawless, youthful, expected. But not quite beautiful.
She marries her law-school boyfriend.
Her life is slender, smooth, punctuated.
Stand next to her and everything makes sense.
The house. Retirement plans. A boy and two girls.
She accents any room she stands in.
She is the dinner-party acquaintance
you never really got to know after all these years.

Only in the last days does she open.
She stops brushing her hair and her dark eyes
have fire in them. The death that grows in her
is not a diminishing, more an unhinging,
the diver's body pausing in the high air,
arced and beautiful before it falls. Suddenly
you feel small before her, unbearably restricted,
as if she had saved a lifetime of abandon
for this one meeting. She takes death as a lover,
hangs out her satin sheets,
stains to the wind.

Never believe the Parson's daughter

No matter how much I clean, the air in this place
still tastes like wet dirt and old orange peels.
The yellow walls are bright as the smell of ammonia
and the face of Sally Ackerson, the goddamn reason
I'm here on a Friday night cleaning the basement
of the Episcopal Church of the Good Shepherd.
Actually it smells more like urine, but no one would ever admit
to noticing that. Not in this church, not in this godforsaken town
where everyone looks around with sharp eyes and tight lips
like they're waiting to say something
that can't be said in public.

If Sally weren't the Parson's daughter
I wouldn't be spending two months worth of Friday nights
like this. Leaky garbage bags and the cruddy old string mop.
I can still see the president of our girls' youth group
as she pulled out the truth in front of everyone:
that one rancid kiss in the storage room.
That one rancid kiss in the stupid rancid urine-stench
of a storage room. One stupid kiss. But good Lord, her mouth,
her sweet young mouth opening wide enough
to pull all my trembling limbs inside.

Sally told her father that I locked her in there
and it was all she could do to fight me off
until he came down to save her.
She'll still believe that when she's forty, when she's married
to that man on the couch and can't figure out what's wrong
or why she hasn't left this Tupperware town.

What more can I learn from this basement?
Mea culpa culpa culpa, I sing as I mop.
The paint is wearing through and the cement floor shines.
Rain on the streets of a new city, it promises.
At the far end of the hall, a door propped open
with a bucket of water. I flick out the fluorescent lights,
follow the dim hallway as far as it leads.

When women were clouds

Back before control top pantyhose,
before the notion of too much woman—
when women were clouds,
we were consulted about everything.
We decided when the ships would sail and if
they would arrive. Men blamed their wet dreams
on the fog. Everyone sketched out secret plans
for a flying machine. It was a good time,
all in all, when women were clouds.
The rain never tasted better. We got more
airtime on the radio and there were many
and better words for women
who put out.

Medusa's lullaby

Medusa, the snakes whisper,
listen, we are making that sound
you love. The sound,
you say, that gives you dreams
of fallen leaves and dead flowers
and the dry hand of someone
who used to be your lover.

Medusa, they whisper,
curling behind her ears
and under her chin
for warmth,
you are still
so young. And already
you have learned to dance
when you are frightened.

Now, let your body be loose,
Medusa. Your cells
are so tightly attached,
relax, move your hips
in circles, move your neck
in circles, let your spine

become sinuous
like us. Soon your skin
will follow, shift
against itself
as you dance.

Listen, it's easy.
We have watched you by the sea,
tracing your slippery shadow
with a stick. This time,
inscribe circles in the sand
with the skin of your belly
until the salty curves
are so familiar, your skin
cannot remember which surface
it is attached to.

Dream densely, Medusella,
we will whisper in your sleep,
but they are coming
and you learn so slowly.
Perhaps our incessant whispering
will be enough, and when they come
for your head, you will know our secrets
and we will leave them

only our skins
and a dry film over empty sockets.
And it will not be you
who will never see again.

Mother Earth at the bar

Out here she doesn't wear Birkenstocks
and cotton dresses. It's Alberta,
after all. Even so, she gets bored
of the bowing down, all those gentle hands.
Come night, she wants to wade
through a mess of hips and eyes
in her finest leather. And she wants to wear it
live: horns, hooves, and fury intact.
She wants to walk into a bar
the way some people walk into a swamp—
everything pushes against her in the dark
and no one cares who she is.
Just for one night she doesn't want to hear
voluptuous, fertile, abundant.
She wants someone to walk up to her
like a forest fire. Say to her:
You fine fat bitch of a woman,
I hope you like it up the ass.

Calling out the wrong name in bed

What can you say? Don't spend your time
denying everything. This woman
could hold you in both hands,
crack and roll you out of your shell
like a hard-boiled egg. In this moment
there is nothing between your skin
and the air. And if you could stay like that,
even for a minute. Let her
turn you over and over
in her hands.

Armpit poem

No one warned her that shame would scuttle up
unannounced, settle in her armpits like a hermit crab,
claiming a used shell. Maybe it's math class:
She raises her hand at a question. Everyone laughs.
It's possible this has nothing to do with the girl and her armpits.
But she feels the small crustacean under her arm,
shielding its eyes against the sudden brightness,
waving its tiny claws as if to pinch out
the fluorescent lights.

In gym class she changes one shirt
under another. She plays soccer with her arms
at her sides. Avoids top shelves, monkey bars,
swimsuits, basketball. At the school dance she anchors
her elbows at her waist, shuffles in that
awkward embrace. And for the most part
she succeeds.

So imagine her surprise that night at the beach.
Summer wind and warm beer. *It's like flying,*
her friend says, arms stretched out at her sides.
Perhaps it's the dark that allows the girl's arms
to open like this, painlessly and without thinking.

Soon, everything she has sidestepped will come
tumbling in. Bench-press, curve ball, slam dunk:
her life will stretch out like a series of questions.
Asking if she is ready to be counted, ready
to wave her hands over her head and be noticed.

But let her have this night. The wind holds her up
and she leans into the world just a little more
than she knows how. Perhaps, she thinks,
the little crab is stretching out of its many-jointed self
as well, floating one small claw on the wind.

Boiled beet

Each Seder is a retelling.
We come together and taste our way
through the story: matzo,
unleavened because fleeing women
can't wait for bread to rise;
charoset, the mortar used
to bind stone together;
bitter herbs, the taste of slavery.
She passes me the haggadah
and I read out loud about the shank bone,
the blood that marked the doors
of Jewish houses with a message
to the angel of death
saying, *Spare this home.*

This year we use a cooked beet
instead, smear beet juice on doorposts
and white picket fences.

I want to run around the city
with a boiled beet, mark the skin
of women everywhere, screaming
may this body

this body
this body
be spared.

Even for a week, I would like
to know we all were safe.
Even for a night.

Morning after

A few hours of uncertainty by the ocean,
that's all. A blueberry seed rolling in the bowl
of an afternoon. But in a world where this summer
is allowed its momentum, I answer questions:
your father? We laughed a lot. He had these eyes.
He knew I was leaving. Before you came along
I wondered what kept me so long, pushed my knee
against his under every table. There I was—
top floor of that old yellow house and summer
gone without me—when you burst in
through the latex. Not a care for our plans.
You always were stubborn, little blue.
I moved clear across the country for you.
Bought winter boots and sold the van with no heat.
There's not a lot can stand in your way, remember that.

I walked to the ocean, bottle in my pocket,
and lay in the matted Crowberry. Four flat pills,
to be taken twelve hours apart. I let the wind
blow my hair into knots. The water was thick with colour.
The sun had made fat blueberries of the summer. The hours
went by one at a time and I spent them as something small
held in the world that would have me. It took most of a day

to swallow the first two. I stayed up late to take the others.
I was lucky: no pain, no nausea, no cramping.
It's not as if I were pregnant. Only two small things
inside me, cancelling each other out. A summer
of suddenly unrelated events falling off a thread like glass beads.
Then I turned to what was left—the van with no heat,
the long highway home, that seedpod of the unhappened
rattling all the way.

Russian doll

Sometimes you twist open the Russian doll
and find the next wooden doll nestled
inside, and another, until there is one so small
that you, a woman without children or even
an abortion to her name, cannot open it.

Sometimes you open the Russian doll
and there is only a miniature bottle
of cheap liquor. A prank, a trick, a hiding place
for something not worthy of concealment.
If you were to unscrew that bottle
you might find the university boyfriend
you once left at a keg party fundraiser.
The hosts hoisting you into a cab as you asked
about the guy in the bathtub. *Don't worry,*
they said, *he'll be fine.* And you just left.
Not telling anyone he was your boyfriend.

You might find any of those events
that could be stories if it weren't for the fact
that they lead nowhere. And thank goodness
for that, really. You can't imagine, good God, and
you've been so careful. No one wants to hear about

the boyfriends you never married, the broken condoms.
It's all so long ago now. But sometimes you forget
how many painted layers there are. And when you arrive
at the last one and you've lost count and you reach
to open it

that's all. You wouldn't call it regret.

This is the summer your mother died and I am leaving in the morning for the city

There's you, sitting in the back of the canoe
beer in your right hand, water to your chest,
orange life jacket riding up around your ears.
Your buddy Paul is in the front seat, his right hand
caught bending one blue and white can
away from the rest of the sixpack floating in his lap.
He looks into the camera with his best
beer-commercial smile, head thrown back into the life jacket
You are laughing too, your head turned slightly
to the left, your sunglasses catching the light.

I let the photo tell its own story.
I don't tell anyone how you begged me not to go back to school,
how I begged you for just one day without your drinking buddies.
That morning we argued all the way to the mainland
with our paddles, me steering for the rocky coast,
you trying to point us toward the Lund pub
where you saw your friend's aluminium skiff.
I don't say I spent our last afternoon
stranded in a pub watching you drink, waiting
for one of your friends to want to go home.
I don't tell how I watched you laughing

in the canoe, drunk and trying to weave through the wake
as we towed you back home.
How I sat in that small metal boat and tried to laugh
with all the guys when you finally leaned too far,
the canoe filling with water
and sinking slowly beneath you.

I just show people this photo.
It's that perfect time of evening:
everyone's skin glows with yellow light.
There are no shadows on any faces.
Even the colour of the life jackets is beautiful.

In which you have not yet and may never

When I think of the ravens now
it's not their beaks, one inside the other,
but the sound—the low rolling caw
that sucked the breath from us
watching in the snow. How it started

suddenly and at its loudest, like adolescence
or the reawakening of grief. Later
you were touching my feet and I think
it scared you a little. The smaller bird
laying its beak flat along the sharpness

of the other's mouth. And the soft call
that undid our ribs, sewed buttons
in our throats. *I can't*, you said,
I can't. But you said it
to the sky.

THE THIN EDGE OF STILLNESS

View from the trailer steps

Everyone I know
is somewhere else.

No one can tell me
what the afternoon means.

In the evening, the moon
rises over the outhouse

not yet full
or broken.

Pass Creek Tower: Arriving

Each year, the uncovering.
The morning like warm dishwater
where the glue dissolves, until you are
one more jar without a label.
In the long afternoon, time
works at your tightly woven minutes
like a stitch-ripper, like rust,
like time. And when the scaffolding
you confuse for yourself
collapses—

Think of it
as two things. First:
getting here. Highways,
hotels, bunkhouses. Cleaning
mouse shit out of cupboards,
making the bed. The trailer
with its three rooms walks you
through the motions—
first chapter of a book, first wet snow,
sleep. Then: a hot cup of tea,
feet on the radio room desk, Irving Layton
cussing about what's important and poetry.

If you were human, you ask yourself.
If you had this day,
and the next—

Inside the teapot, small
bound-up balls of leaves uncatch
in hot water. Every corner
turns the colour of tea. Outside,
the tower rises above the trees
and gets in the way
of the weather.

Tower time

Time is money, and pink
is the new black. Or maybe
it's orange. What would I know?
I'm reading old magazines
and counting the rain. Out here,
this is all I can tell you: solar shower
is the new makeover, voice is the new touch.
Rain is currency, gossip, hall pass.
Clouds are the new opera. And time—
well. No matter what I try, time
won't wear anyone's hand-me-downs.
It just wants to run around naked in the yard
all bloody day.

The smell of heat

1. FIVE DEGREES

Somewhere a man with expensive eyeglasses
parses the smell of water
from a shelf of small clear tubes.
He is precise and the perfume
will keep its scent, even
when it dries.
This is true.
Also: it costs a lot of money.
But you won't understand that now.
This day. Dew like birthright.
Ditches and driveways
with their flat, shiny puddles.
Wet skin of the morning. The wrist
of it. The neck.

2. NINETEEN DEGREES

You want to dip your fingers into something
and lick them: thumb finger finger finger finger.
Cottonwood. Tall grass heating in the afternoon.
That place from your childhood, the one
you remember by smell, is just around the
corner. Every corner.
This one. Surely
this one.

Government man calls the forest *logs*.
We have to save the logs, he says.

Lightning looks down with its big dry mouth:
Tinder. Kindling. Hard little nipples of wood.

All those names and no shade.
You test the thin edge of stillness against your finger.

Black spruce, aspen, lodgepole, birch.
Timber. Cutblock. Fuel-type—

I'll call you whatever you want if you take off your shirt.
Say it for me:

       Greed. Fingers. Precipice. Pine-pitch. Ignition.

Cabin fever

If I had a bottle of wine up here, I'd hold the neck in my fist and tip it up too fast. Let the weight of it rip through the long dusty day right to my feet. Like rain. Or a road. Or somewhere to go.

If I had a bottle of wine, I'd lie on the ground and practise at happy drunk. Despite a hundred feet of good ladder and the thrill of distance in the dark. Or that place under the hatch where the ladder cage opens to the sky and you lean back, harnessless, into it. *Because you can't climb with a bottle in your hand*, I'd say. Knowing a thousand famous men have proven me wrong.

Or I'd sit here and love this place like they would. All the good trees. Fireweed tender as a second chance, not knowing what came before. The things men tell each other when they're drunk. How conversation, even love, becomes a ladder, and they climb anything that goes up.

Hammock, I'd think. Sky. Runaway sun. I could eat corn and run open-mouthed and greasy into the woods where the sun went. Maybe it's simple as a picnic table with a pot of boiling corn. Easy as forgetting my fear of the strangers who roll up my driveway at dusk. Waving them closer with butter on my hands, grease stains on my pants where I wipe off my palms. *Corn*, I'd say, kernels filling my mouth. A mouth full of perfect days. The butter ground down to the bottom of its thin metal wrapper. The endless shucking of corn.

I could love this place right. Serve up summer night like fall-apart homemade dessert. But before I do, I find Al Purdy's already chewed it up and spat it out perfect, and I hate him for it. *Running and running naked with summer in your mouth.* Fuck you, Al Purdy. I run my teeth over the kernels of all my favourites. Wanting to see them suffer. But no. They do that already. So beautifully.

It seems they are always drinking. Or undoing the drinking of their past. The hard glamour of damage. Polished like infidelity, like leaving. *Why try?* I think. When they've already been here so much better and drunker and more foolish with love.

I turn to offer them more corn, but they're gone. Have thrown their husks on the grass and called it beautiful. Even laughter is a ladder. Have left their garbage and taken my truck. Are drinking my wine a bottle each like beer. Are looking for another roadside stand. *Hey,* I yell, *but it's twenty cents a cob and six for a buck.* It's summer. It's corn. It's so fucking cheap. They hold a twenty out the window and watch it flap. Six for a dollar. One good hot night. Somewhere to go. Corn. Corn so sweet you eat it raw. Windows cranked. Gasoline. That perfect speed that comes with its own warm wind.

Pass Creek Tower: Solstice

We fill our bathtubs from our rain barrels,
build separate fires below them. But all day
I've watched her weather come through.
Storm cells tracking southeast toward me
and then passing to my north.
How fast it comes each year, we tell each other
on matching cordless phones.
The garden barely a month planted
and it's the longest day.

I'll call back when it's lit, I say.
There aren't many
I can tell my aloneness to
without making it smaller:
sourdough rising in a bowl,
my dogs asleep in a cardboard box,
how I build a fire.

In my yard the pea shoots are six inches
and have yet to find anything
to hold on to. Later, I know,
the peas will find the trellis
and outgrow it. Will hang off into the air

threatening to pull the whole thing down.

But that comes after. Tonight
is simply the end of the longest day.
Soon we'll slip into our steaming tubs,
lie waiting late into the night for some stars.
The sun has done its hard work
of melting ice, warming rock and soil,
heating the spark of green until the bud
breaks. Now even the shorter
and shorter days will be enough
to feed the momentum of heat.

There will be apples and forest fires.
There will be dry lightning and helicopters
towing buckets of water behind them
in the hot air. Heatwaves, high hazard days,
fires smouldering under even the first snow.
It is motion already, all of it. Even what seems,
in this moment, unthinkable. The forest will burn
for a while. Then we will leave. We don't know
when, but sure as night, the trucks will arrive
to take us back to town as they do each year.
And one day we will hold truth in our mouths
like water.

Perhaps we, who have been trying
so hard, who have been looking and looking
all these long days, can rest. Perhaps later,
the thing we struggled for will reach out
and touch us softly. Its small new fingers.
Which is to say, I tell her before we hang up,
remind me. When the days are short,
remind me how late we stayed up
just wanting some stars—

Money clouds

Watch them cram against the horizon
like girls in cheap push-up bras
rushing the stage. Swelling up and spilling
over ridge after ridge. And then—
rain. Rain like a door closing in, shutting out
whatever distance has made you weary.
The pauses before the thunder get shorter:
twenty kilometres, now ten. You try not to count.
But the mountains take their cut, and those ridges,
and the clouds spit past, nothing
but a hard shoulder of wind. They drift east,
spent, and not giving a rat's ass what kind of show
you had in mind. Forget the rain barrel and the thought
of water for a bath, the way the air smells
after a storm. The roads will keep their dust,
the sky its haze. And when the storm passes, you sit
on your doorstep—waiting for something, watching it

leave. Unwilling, though you look up to the sky, to say
you thought someone might have come along by now.
Unable to retrace your muddy tracks out of here.
Instead, thinking: rain, thunder. Thinking rain,
goddammit, enough rain, and you'd be clean.

Mackerel sky

Today, finally, I see the thick-legged spider
that has been attaching its single strands
to my fire tower. Some reach forty feet
into the wind and hang there.
One floats level with my window, ripples slowly.
It crosses briefly above another and returns to its place
without tangling. What are they for?
They will never reach the trees below, or the ground.
As the wind dies, they begin to sink and when it picks up
they rise again, horizontal, as if suspended in a slow-moving current.

Above, the rows of mackerel sky stretch out
like the wide sweep of a hand indicating all
that can be seen: this and this and this.

Here is the border of a place we don't come from
and won't return to. A surface we will not break above,
shaking ourselves like swimming dogs. What then?
The curling rows like orderly fish. No, no:
they are part of something that can only
be understood as order from a distance. Point blank,
it's sleek muscle and quiet splash, the arc above and dip
below, the glint, oh—each one briefly—here I am, here.

They will never see the smooth shape,
the fantastic creature they make, the lines swelling and shrinking
and curving across the sky without breaking, but they
continue to jump again and again. Simply to leap

a fish-length of the distance
to the sun. Those thousands of light years—
it doesn't matter. Whatever you have done today
is enough.

Here we are, the clouds floating on our pocket of air
as if gas were simply a thinner liquid,
as if we were exactly where we belong.
As if—minnowing through our small lives
and occasionally lifting our faces to the sky—
it were enough. As if this:
the spider and its long impossible threads hanging in the air,
catching the watery light now, and losing it. As if this
and this and this and this.

Time to go

You sit in the windless hollow behind the house,
listen to pine needles sift through your fingers.

We chose what to take. The first time
in three months we agreed about anything.
We managed to load it in the car
without discussing whose photographs,
whose books, whose car.

Half a town away the fires
are walking slowly, unquietly
toward us. They taste whole houses.
The hot air alone could knock you over.

And the wind: even to the child
it might pluck from the funnel of a tornado,
and place gently on the corrugated wreck
of the old arena, the wind is no friend.

You went to the gully for shade.
Now your hands are full of fuel.
I watch you walk slowly back to the car,
as if to run might draw too much attention.

As if to avoid even the smallest
friction.

You open your hands and a soft wind
takes the needles. Quieter
than kerosene from an eyedropper,
they settle on the path.

Time to go, you say.
Yes.

Pass Creek Tower: Equinox

Last bath of the season.
Head back on the ledge of the tub,
ribs on the surface like frets, and
a breeze the exact temperature
of slide guitar. It was the kind of moment
I wanted even while I still had it. Every kind of open-
handed longing: the *again! again!* of perfect stillness.
Wanting and having: the harmonics of that.
Waiting to see which note would last
longer.

Under me, the coals still smouldering.
Above me, a moon the size of a small sky.
When I got hot, I draped my legs
steaming over each side of the tub.
The garden had come so close.
My left foot met pea flowers, pea shoots, fat green peas.
Tangled itself in those small green tendrils
that reach into the air for something to grow on.
Five months and it was the first time
I'd been touched by the world. Handshakes,
forestry officers, grocery deliveries, but not
this. Gentle. Unexpected. Eyes closed,

then open, then closed.
My body a ladle of bathwater held up
to the mouth of the sky.

A new theory of darkness

Before the crows,
evening. They come a few at first,
then many, and when their wings touch
and lose their lines against the sky,
night.

I used to think this was how
darkness came: in pieces, falling together like a
jagged-winged jigsaw. Each bird obliterating
a wingspan's worth of sky. Darkness
merely a fitting together, a density.

And whatever imperfections
we called stars,
just the blue mirror of feathers
catching our light.

ACKNOWLEDGEMENTS

I am grateful for the assistance of the Newfoundland and Labrador Arts Council, BC Arts Council, City of St. John's, The Banff Centre, and The Wallace Stegner House.

Earlier versions of these poems have appeared in various journals and anthologies, including *The Antigonish Review, ARC, CV2, Grain, The Inner Harbour Review, The Malahat Review, Prairie Fire, PRISM International, Room, The Torah: A Women's Commentary, Joining the Sisterhood: Young Jewish Women Write Their Lives*, and *The Best Canadian Poetry in English 2008*. Thank you to the editors of these publications, and to everyone who keeps them alive.

The first section is for the people who stood by me when I was sick, and for everyone whose lives have been changed by illness.

The third section is for the fire towers and lookouts of Alberta, and for my dog friends Oscar and Lambert who kept me company out in the woods.

Thank you to Halli Villegas for her vision, to Shirarose Wilensky for her patience and careful editing, and to everyone at Tightrope Books. Thank you to Vivienne McMaster for the author photo.

To Ariel Gordon, Bren Simmers, Degan Davis, Elena Johnson, Jill Wigmore, and Lisa Baird who read and helped edit substantial portions of this work—this book would not exist as it does without you. My gratitude.

Thank you also to Lorna Crozier for her generosity of spirit and teaching, to Tim Lilburn for his support, to Rabbi David Mivisair for deepening my understanding of the opening quote, to Val for being there since the dead poet days, and to my parents who sang me to sleep with old poems and drunken sailor songs.